KEYS TO HANDLING YOUR EMOTION:

The ultimate guide on how to handle your emotions

BAKER Ralph

Table of contents

Chapter 1

What are emotions

Emotions may be characterized as psychological states that encompass thoughts and emotions, physiological changes, expressive actions, and desires to act. The specific mix of these factors varies from emotion to emotion, and feelings may or may not be accompanied by overt actions. This complex of feelings and actions is prompted by an event that is either experienced or remembered. Someone insults you. Depending on the nature of the insult and your sense of the amount to which it was or was not meant to offend you, you can feel furious or irritated. If you feel furious, your cheeks may redden, your heart may beat faster, your hands tighten, and thoughts of retaliation arise to you. In certain circumstances, you could take action against the offensive individual. Days later, remembering the insult may re-evoke at least some characteristics of the initial emotional response. Similarly, clear-cut instances of feeling might be offered for fear, pleasure, love, contempt, and melancholy, among many others. However, other emotions are less clear-cut, in that they do not necessarily include changes in physiological or motivational states and do not always result in behavioral change. Take the case of regret. Having made a choice or adopted a course of action that ends out poorly, one may well feel profound regret, but this subjective experience will generally not be accompanied by changes in physiology or behavior.

Further complexities occur when evaluating psychological states that appear to be borderline instances of emotion: physical pain, generalized or free-floating worry, sexual excitation, boredom, sadness, and impatience, all of which might be considered as examples of affective states. Psychologists who research emotion prefer to discriminate between affective experiences that have a distinct object and those that do not, claiming that emotion is a word that should be reserved for psychological states that have an object. On this premise, chronic pain, general states of boredom, despair, or anger would not be categorized as emotions, but sexual arousal—to the degree that it has a distinct object— would be considered as an emotional state. The divide between affective states that have an object and those that do not differentiate emotions, on one side, from moods (e.g., irritation, boredom) and affective dispositions (depression, generalized anxiety), on the other.

Recognizing the difficulties inherent in trying to arrive at watertight definitions of what constitutes an emotion, theorists are generally agreed regarding emotion as a set of states that has a fuzzy boundary with other psychological states, such as beliefs, attitudes, values, moods, and personality dispositions. What is not in question is that the collection of states labeled emotion is characterized by excellent examples, such as rage, fear, and intense love. Where there is space for debate, at or around the fuzzy border with surrounding states, psychologists are often preoccupied with whether the state in question is an emotion. The challenge of identifying emotion is therefore finessed.

Emotions History and Background

Modern emotion theory is commonly traced back to the works of Charles Darwin or William James. Writing in the second half of the 19th century, these writers concentrated on themes that are still the subject of investigation and discussion almost 150 years later. Darwin's concentration was on the link between subjective feeling and overt conduct. He believed that three principles explain the link between emotions and expressive action. Of them, the first, the principle of useful related habits, is the one most usually connected to Darwinian theories for expressive behavior. Here the notion is that movements of the face that once had a function during emotional experiences have become automatic accompaniments of such feelings. Thus, the frowning that commonly follows anger could serve to protect the eye socket by pushing the brows forward and together, while the eye-widening that typically accompanies astonishment might aid to take in more visual information when rapid, unfamiliar occurrences occur. Surprisingly, considering the overall theory of evolution for which Darwin is better known, his works on emotional expression did not describe this expression as the consequence of a process of natural selection. Rather, he regarded the emotion-expression relationship as a learned habit that subsequently is passed on to one's descendants. However, the contemporary evolutionary theory may simply be applied to this dilemma, resulting in the notion that it was the adaptive relevance for the individual or the community that led to emotions being externally expressed. The concept that there is a strong link between emotional experience and physical manifestation is surely one that is mirrored in current emotion theory.

James focused on the basic subject of the determinants of emotion. James advocated what has come to be called a peripheral theory of emotion, in which he argued that the perception of an arousing stimulus causes changes in peripheral organs, such as the viscera (heart, lungs, stomach, etc.) and the voluntary muscles, and that emotion is quite simply the perception of these bodily changes. To borrow James's example, it is not that people tremble and flee because they are terrified; rather, they are afraid because they tremble and run. This begs the issue of how the physical changes come about. Here James argued for a direct relationship between perception and physiological change, using the analogy of a lock and a key. The fit between the perception of emotion-arousing stimuli and the human mind is, in James's perspective, such that the stimuli automatically unlock physiological changes in the body, and it is the experience of these changes that is the emotion. The concept that there is a tight relationship between perception and emotion, largely unmediated by conscious cognition, is still evident in current emotion theory, as is the notion that changes in the peripheral activity of the body lead to changes in emotion.

A key plank in the theoretical analysis of emotion in psychology occurred with the emergence of cognitivism (i.e., close study of mental processes) in the 1960s. The first proponent of a notion that came to be known as appraisal theory was Magda Arnold. She suggested that what makes individuals feel emotion is not physiological change, but rather the cognitive process that makes one form of stimuli emotionally stimulating while another kind of stimulus leaves them chilly. The distinction, she claimed, is that the emotionally aroused experience is personally relevant and important to individuals. Unless the stimulation matters to them, they will not get emotional. What matters to one person may leave another person cold. This emphasis on subjective meaning in appraisal theory led researchers to shift their attention from the objective properties of emotional stimuli to the subjective processes (appraisal processes) by which perceivers attach significance and meaning to stimuli. Modern emotion theory is very much concerned with this process of meaning-making.

Notice that these three key sources of influence on modern emotion theory map rather neatly onto three of the supposed components of emotion: expression, physiological activity, and cognitions. Before analyzing each of these three components in further depth, explore the link between emotion and social psychology.

Emotions are a subject researched within numerous subdisciplines of psychology, including clinical psychology, biological psychology, and developmental psychology. Yet if one studies the history of psychological thought and research on emotion, it is evident that social psychologists have played a key role. In one way this is shocking. There are emotional responses that have little or nothing to do with the social reality that is the major interest of social psychologists: Think of dread of heights, snakes, or grizzly bears. Yet these sentiments are not representative of the variety of emotions that individuals experience in ordinary life. As indicated previously, emotions are usually about something: They have an object. This item is very frequently social. It is a person (a competitor for your loved one's attention), a social group (an organization that conducts inspirational work in undeveloped nations), a social event (your favorite sports team winning a trophy), or a social or cultural product (a piece of music) (a piece of music). It turns out that these social things are far more likely than nonsocial objects to be the cause of our daily emotions.

Furthermore, many emotions are either intrinsically or functionally social, in the sense that they either would not be experienced in the absence of others or appear to have no other purpose than to link individuals to other people. Emotions such as compassion, sympathy, maternal love, adoration, and appreciation rely on other people being physically or mentally present. Fear of rejection, loneliness, humiliation, remorse, shame, envy, and sexual attraction are emotions that appear to have their major purpose in seeking out or solidifying social connections

Chapter 2

Ways to regulate your emotions

The capacity to feel and express emotions is more vital than you may imagine.

As the emotional response to a specific event, emotions play a significant influence in your responses. When you're in touch with them, you have access to critical information that assists with:

decision-making\relationship success
day-to-day interactions
self-care
While emotions may play a positive function in your everyday life, they can take a toll on your mental health and interpersonal relationships when they start to seem out of control.

Vicki Botnick, a therapist in Tarzana, California, notes that any feeling — even euphoria, delight, or others you'd generally see as good — may escalate to a point where it becomes impossible to regulate.

With a little work, however, you can take back the controls. Two research from 2010Trusted Source shows that having high emotional control abilities is associated with well-being. Plus, the second one discovered a probable correlation between these talents and financial success, so putting in some effort on that front may pay off. Here are some tips to get you started.

How to improve intellect using your emotions

The capacity to feel and express emotions is more vital than you may imagine.

As the emotional response to a specific event, emotions play a significant influence in your responses. When you're in touch with them, you have access to critical information that assists with:

With a little work, however, you can take back the controls. Two research from 2010Trusted Source shows that having high emotional control abilities is associated with well-being. Plus, the second one discovered a probable correlation between these talents and financial success, so putting in some effort on that front may pay off.

Here are some tips to get you started.

1. Take a look at the influence of your emotions

Intense emotions aren't all negative.

"Emotions make our life intriguing, distinctive, and vibrant," Botnick adds. "Strong sensations might suggest that we accept life wholeheartedly, that we're not denying our natural reactions."

It's entirely natural to suffer some emotional overflow on occasion— when something fantastic occurs, when something tragic happens, when you feel like you've missed out.

So, how do you tell when there's a problem?

Emotions that routinely go out of control could lead to:

. Relationship or friendship conflict\s. trouble connecting to others\s. difficulties in job or school\s. an impulse to take drugs to assist control your emotions physical or emotional outbursts

Find some time to take stock of precisely how your uncontrolled emotions are influencing your day-to-day living. This will make it easy to identify problem areas (measure your progress) (and track your success).

2. Aim for regulation, not repression

You can't manage your emotions with a dial (if it were that simple!). But suppose, for a minute, if you could regulate emotions this way.

You wouldn't want to keep them running at maximum all the time. You also wouldn't want to shut them off totally, though.

When you suppress or repress emotions, you're blocking yourself from experiencing and expressing them. This might happen intentionally (suppression) or subconsciously (repression) (repression).

Either may lead to mental and physical health issues, including:

. anxiety\s depression\s. sleep issues\s. muscular strain and pain\s. trouble handling stress\s. drug usage

3. Identify what you're experiencing
Taking a minute to check in with yourself about your emotions will help you begin getting back in control.

Say you've been seeing someone for a few months. You tried booking a date last week, but they indicated they didn't have time. Yesterday, you texted again, adding, "I'd want to meet you soon. Can you meet this week?"

They eventually react, more than a day later: "Can't. Busy."

You're suddenly terribly agitated. Without pausing to think, you fling your phone across the room, knock over your wastebasket, and kick your desk, stubbing your toe.

Interrupt yourself by asking:

.

.What am I experiencing right now? (disappointed, perplexed, indignant)

.What occurred to make me feel this way? (They blew me off with no explanation.)

. Does the circumstance have an alternate explanation that would make sense? (Maybe they're worried, unwell, or coping with something else they don't feel comfortable sharing. They could aim to explain more when they can.)

. What do I want to do about these feelings? (Scream, release my rage by tossing stuff, send back something unpleasant.)

. Is there a better method of dealing with them? (Ask whether everything's OK. Ask when they're free next. Go for a stroll or run.)

By examining different alternatives, you're reframing your thinking, which might help you adjust your original extreme response.

It might take some time before this reaction becomes a habit. With experience, going through these processes in your thoughts will become simpler (and more successful) (and more effective).

4. Accept your feelings – all of them

If you're attempting to grow better at controlling emotions, you can try downplaying your sentiments to yourself.

When you hyperventilate after hearing wonderful news or fall on the floor screaming and weeping when you can't locate your keys, it can seem beneficial to tell yourself, "Just calm down," or "It's not that big of an issue, so don't panic out."

But this invalidates your experience. It is a significant thing to you.

Accepting emotions as they arrive helps you grow more comfortable with them. Increasing your comfort with overwhelming emotions helps you to completely experience them without responding in severe, unproductive ways.

Accepting emotions as they arrive helps you grow more comfortable with them. Increasing your comfort with overwhelming emotions helps you to completely experience them without responding in severe, unproductive ways.

5. Keep a mood diary
Writing down (or typing out) your emotions and the reactions they cause might help you discover any disruptive tendencies.

Sometimes, it's enough to mentally trace feelings back via your thoughts. Putting sentiments into paper might help you to ponder on them more profoundly.

It also helps you realize when particular conditions, like problems at work or family strife, lead to harder-to-control emotions. Identifying particular triggers makes it feasible to come up with solutions to handle them more successfully.

Journaling delivers the greatest value when you do it every day. Keep your diary with you and write down powerful emotions or sensations as they happen. Try to notice the triggers and your response. If your reply didn't assist, utilize your notebook to explore more beneficial alternatives for the future.. Take a deep breath

There's plenty to be said about the power of a deep breath, whether you're wildly joyful or so upset you can't speak.

Slowing down and paying attention to your breath won't make the feelings go away (and remember, that's not the purpose).
Still, deep breathing exercises may help you center yourself and take a step back from the initial acute flash of emotion and any excessive response you wish to avoid.

The next time you sense emotions beginning to take control:

6.. Breathe in gently. Deep breaths originate from the diaphragm, not the chest. It may help too. envision your breath rising from deep in your belly.\s. Hold it. Hold your breath for a count of three, then let it out slowly.\s. Consider a mantra. Some individuals find it beneficial to repeat a mantra, such as "I am calm" or "I am relaxed."

7. Know when to express yourself

There's a time and place for everything,\s even deep emotions. Sobbing uncontrollably is a relatively frequent reaction to losing a loved one, for example. Screaming into your pillow, even hitting it, could help you express some rage and anxiety after being rejected.

Other instances, though, call for some moderation. No matter how furious you are, yelling at your supervisor over an unjust disciplinary action won't help.

Being attentive to your surroundings and the circumstance might help you understand when it's OK to let emotions out and when you might want to sit with them for the time.

8. Give yourself some space

Getting some space from overwhelming sensations might help you make sure you're responding to them in sensible ways, according to Botnick.

This distance could be physical, like leaving a distressing environment, for example. But you may also establish some mental space by diverting yourself. While you don't want to ignore or avoid emotions totally, it's not bad to divert yourself until you're in a better situation to deal with them. Just make sure you do come back to them. Healthy distractions are only brief.

Try:

taking a walk\swatching a hilarious video\stalking to a loved one\spending a few minutes with your pet

9. Try meditation

If you practice meditation already, it could be one of your go-to ways of dealing with overwhelming emotions.

Meditation may help you expand your awareness of all emotions and events. When you meditate, you're training yourself to sit with those emotions, to observe them without criticizing yourself or seeking to alter them or make them go away.
As indicated above, learning to accept all of your feelings helps make emotional management simpler. Meditation helps you strengthen those accepting abilities. It also has additional advantages, including helping you relax and feel better

10. Stay on top of stress

When you're under a lot of stress, controlling your emotions might become more challenging. Even persons who typically can regulate their emotions effectively could find it tougher in times of intense tension and stress.

Reducing stress, or finding more effective methods to handle it, might help your emotions become more bearable.

Mindfulness activities like meditation may assist with stress, too. They won't get rid of it, but they can make it simpler to live with.

Other good strategies to deal with stress include:

getting adequate sleep\smaking time to converse (and laugh) with friends\sexercise spending time in nature\making time for leisure and interests.

11. Talk to a therapist

If your emotions continue to seem overpowering, it may be time to seek professional assistance.

Long-term or chronic emotional dysregulation and mood fluctuations are connected to various mental health problems, including borderline personality disorder and bipolar disorder. Trouble managing emotions may also connect to trauma, familial troubles, or other underlying concerns, Botnick notes.

A therapist may give sympathetic, judgment-free assistance as you:

identify variables leading to dysregulated emotions address severe mood swings\s learn how to down-regulate intense feelings or up-regulate limited emotional expression\practice challenging and reframing feelings that cause distress\sMood swings and intense emotions can provoke negative or unwanted thoughts that eventually trigger feelings of hopelessness or despair.

This loop might ultimately lead to maladaptive coping mechanisms like self-harm or even thoughts of death. If you begin thinking about suicide or have cravings for self-harm, speak to a trustworthy loved one who can help you obtain assistance quickly

Chapter 3

How to control your emotions, so your emotions don't control you

Have you ever said something out of anger that you later regretted? Do you let fear talk you out of taking the risks that could really benefit you? If so, you're not alone.

Emotions are powerful. Your mood determines how you interact with people, how much money you spend, how you deal with challenges, and how you spend your time.

Gaining control over your emotions will help you become mentally stronger. Fortunately, anyone can become better at regulating their emotions. Just like any other skill, managing your emotions requires practice and dedication.

Managing your emotions isn't the same as suppressing them. Ignoring your sadness or pretending you don't feel pain won't make those emotions go away.

In fact, unaddressed emotional wounds are likely to get worse over time. And there's a good chance suppressing your feelings will cause you to turn to unhealthy coping skills--like food or alcohol.

It's important to acknowledge your feelings while also recognizing that your emotions don't have to control you. If you wake up on the wrong side of the bed, you can take control of your mood and turn your day around. If you are angry, you can choose to calm yourself down.

Here are three ways to gain better control over your mood:

Before you can change how you feel, you need to acknowledge what you're experiencing right now. Are you nervous? Do you feel disappointed? Are you sad?

Keep in mind that anger sometimes masks emotions that feel vulnerable--like shame or embarrassment. So pay close attention to what's really going on inside of you.

Put a name to your emotions. Keep in mind you might feel a whole bunch of emotions at once--like anxious, frustrated, and impatient.

Labeling how you feel can take a lot of the sting out of the emotion. It can also help you take careful note of how those feelings are likely to affect your decisions.

Your emotions affect the way you perceive events. If you're feeling anxious and you get an email from the boss that says she wants to see you right away, you might assume you're going to get fired. If however, you're feeling happy when you get that same email, your first thought might be that you're going to be promoted or congratulated on a job well done.

Consider the emotional filter you're looking at the world through. Then, reframe your thoughts to develop a more realistic view.

If you catch yourself thinking, "This networking event is going to be a complete waste of time. No one is going to talk to me and I'm going to look like an idiot," remind yourself, "It's up to me to get something out of the event. I'llintroduce myself to new people and show interest in learning about them."

•

Sometimes, the easiest way to gain a different perspective is to take a step back and ask yourself, "What would I say to a friend who had this problem?" Answering that question will take some of the emotion out of the equation so you can think more rationally.

•

If you find yourself dwelling on negative things, you may need to change the channel in your brain. A quick physical activity, like going for a walk or cleaning off your desk, can help you stop ruminating.

•

When you're in a bad mood, you're likely to engage in activities that keep you in that state of mind. Isolating yourself, mindlessly scrolling through your phone, or complaining to people around you are just a few of the typical "go-to bad mood behaviors" you might indulge in.

But, those things will keep you stuck. You have to take positive action if you want to feel better.

•

Think of the things you do when you feel happy. Do those things when you're in a bad mood and you'll start to feel better.

•

Here are a few examples of mood boosters:

•

Call a friend to talk about something pleasant (not to continue complaining).

Go for a walk.

Meditate for a few minutes.

Listen to uplifting music.

Managing your emotions is tough at times. And there will likely be a specific emotion--like anger--that sometimes gets the best of you.

But the more time and attention you spend on regulating your emotions, the mentally stronger you'll become. You'll gain confidence in your ability to handle discomfort while also knowing that you can make healthy choices that shift your mood.

Chapter 4

How to grow intelligence using your emotions

What is emotional intelligence or EQ?
Emotional intelligence (otherwise known as emotional quotient or EQ) is the ability to understand, use, and manage your own emotions in positive ways to relieve stress, communicate effectively, empathize with others, overcome challenges and defuse conflict. Emotional intelligence helps you build stronger relationships, succeed at school and work, and achieve your career and personal goals. It can also help you to connect with your feelings, turn intention into action, and make informed decisions about what matters most to you.

Emotional intelligence is commonly defined by four attributes:

Self-management – You're able to control impulsive feelings and behaviors, manage your emotions in healthy ways, take initiative, follow through on commitments, and adapt to changing circumstances.

Self-awareness – You recognize your own emotions and how they affect your thoughts and behavior. You know your strengths and weaknesses, and have self-confidence.
Social awareness – You have empathy. You can understand the emotions, needs, and concerns of other people, pick up on emotional cues, feel comfortable socially, and recognize the power dynamics in a group or organization.
Relationship management – You know how to develop and maintain good relationships, communicate clearly, inspire and influence others, work well in a team, and manage conflict

Why is emotional intelligence so important?
As we know, it's not the smartest people who are the most successful or the most fulfilled in life. You probably know people who are academically brilliant and yet are socially inept and unsuccessful at work or in their personal relationships. Intellectual ability or your intelligence quotient (IQ) isn't enough on its own to achieve success in life. Yes, your IQ can help you get into college, but it's your EQ that will help you manage the stress and emotions when facing your final exams. IQ and EQ exist in tandem and are most effective when they build off one another.

Emotional intelligence affects:
Your performance at school or work. High emotional intelligence can help you navigate the social complexities of the workplace, lead and motivate

others, and excel in your career. In fact, when it comes to gauging important job candidates, many companies now rate emotional intelligence as important as technical ability and employ EQ testing before hiring.

Your physical health. If you're unable to manage your emotions, you are probably not managing your stress either. This can lead to serious health problems. Uncontrolled stress raises blood pressure, suppresses the immune system, increases the risk of heart attacks and strokes, contributes to infertility, and speeds up the aging process. The first step to improving emotional intelligence is to learn how to manage stress.

Your mental health. Uncontrolled emotions and stress can also impact your mental health, making you vulnerable to anxiety and depression. If you are unable to understand, get comfortable with, or manage your emotions, you'll also struggle to form strong relationships. This in turn can leave you feeling lonely and isolated and further exacerbate any mental health problems.

Your relationships. By understanding your emotions and how to control them, you're better able to express how you feel and understand how others are feeling. This allows you to communicate more effectively and forge stronger relationships, both at work and in your personal life.

Your social intelligence. Being in tune with your emotions serves a social purpose, connecting you to other people and the world around you. Social intelligence enables you to recognize friend from foe, measure another person's interest in you, reduce stress, balance your nervous system through social communication, and feel loved and happy.

Building emotional intelligence: Four key skills to increasing your EQ

The skills that make up emotional intelligence can be learned at any time. However, it's important to remember that there is a difference between simply learning about EQ and applying that knowledge to your life. Just because you know you should do something doesn't mean you will—especially when you become overwhelmed by stress, which can override your best intentions. In order to permanently change behavior in ways that stand up under pressure, you need to learn how to overcome stress in the moment, and in your relationships, in order to remain emotionally aware.

The key skills for building your EQ and improving your ability to manage emotions and connect with others are:

Self-management
Self-awareness
Social awareness

Relationship management

Building emotional intelligence, key skill 1: Self-management

In order for you to engage your EQ, you must be able to use your emotions to make constructive decisions about your behavior. When you become overly stressed, you can lose control of your emotions and the ability to act thoughtfully and appropriately.

Think about a time when stress has overwhelmed you. Was it easy to think clearly or make a rational decision? Probably not. When you become overly stressed, your ability to both think clearly and accurately assess emotions—your own and other people's—becomes compromised

Emotions are important pieces of information that tell you about yourself and others, but in the face of stress that takes us out of our comfort zone, we can become overwhelmed and lose control of ourselves. With the ability to manage stress and stay emotionally present, you can learn to receive upsetting information without letting it override your thoughts and self-control. You'll be able to make choices that allow you to control impulsive feelings and behaviors, manage your emotions in healthy ways, take initiative, follow through on commitments, and adapt to changing circumstances.

Key skill 2: Self-awareness

Managing stress is just the first step to building emotional intelligence. The science of attachment indicates that your current emotional experience is likely a reflection of your early life experience. Your ability to manage core feelings such as anger, sadness, fear, and joy often depends on the quality and consistency of your early life emotional experiences. If your primary caretaker as an infant understood and valued your emotions, it's likely your emotions have become valuable assets in adult life. But, if your emotional experiences as an infant were confusing, threatening or painful, it's likely you've tried to distance yourself from your emotions.

But being able to connect to your emotions—having a moment-to-moment connection with your changing emotional experience—is the key to understanding how emotion influences your thoughts and actions.

Do you experience feelings that flow, encountering one emotion after another as your experiences change from moment to moment?

Are your emotions accompanied by physical sensations that you experience in places like your stomach, throat, or chest?

Do you experience individual feelings and emotions, such as anger, sadness, fear, and joy, each of which is evident in subtle facial expressions?

Can you experience intense feelings that are strong enough to capture both your attention and that of others?

Do you pay attention to your emotions? Do they factor into your decision making?

If any of these experiences are unfamiliar, you may have "turned down" or "turned off" your emotions. In order to build EQ—and become emotionally healthy—you must reconnect to your core emotions, accept them, and become comfortable with them. You can achieve this through the practice of mindfulness.

Mindfulness is the practice of purposely focusing your attention on the present moment—and without judgment. The cultivation of mindfulness has roots in Buddhism, but most religions include some type of similar prayer or meditation technique. Mindfulness helps shift your preoccupation with thought toward an appreciation of the moment, your physical and emotional sensations, and brings a larger perspective on life. Mindfulness calms and focuses you, making you more self-aware in the process.

Key skill 3: Social awareness

Social awareness enables you to recognize and interpret the mainly nonverbal cues others are constantly using to communicate with you. These cues let you know how others are really feeling, how their emotional state is changing from moment to moment, and what's truly important to them.

When groups of people send out similar nonverbal cues, you're able to read and understand the power dynamics and shared emotional experiences of the group. In short, you're empathetic and socially comfortable.

Mindfulness is an ally of emotional and social awareness

To build social awareness, you need to recognize the importance of mindfulness in the social process. After all, you can't pick up on subtle nonverbal cues when you're in your own head, thinking about other things, or simply zoning out on your phone. Social awareness requires your presence in the moment. While many of us pride ourselves on an ability to multitask, this means that you'll miss the subtle emotional shifts taking place in other people that help you fully understand them.

You are actually more likely to further your social goals by setting other thoughts aside and focusing on the interaction itself.

Following the flow of another person's emotional responses is a give-and-take process that requires you to also pay attention to the changes in your own emotional experience.

Paying attention to others doesn't diminish your own self-awareness. By investing the time and effort to really pay attention to others, you'll actually gain insight into your own emotional state as well as your values and beliefs. For example, if you feel discomfort hearing others express certain views, you'll have learned something important about yourself

Key skill 4: Relationship management

Working well with others is a process that begins with emotional awareness and your ability to recognize and understand what other people are experiencing. Once emotional awareness is in play, you can effectively develop additional social/emotional skills that will make your relationships more effective, fruitful, and fulfilling.

Become aware of how effectively you use nonverbal communication. It's impossible to avoid sending nonverbal messages to others about what you think and feel. The many muscles in the face, especially those around the eyes, nose, mouth and forehead, help you to wordlessly convey your own emotions as well as read other peoples' emotional intent. The emotional part of your brain is always on—and even if you ignore its messages—others won't. Recognizing the nonverbal messages that you send to others can play a huge part in improving your relationships.

Use humor and play to relieve stress. Humor, laughter and play are natural antidotes to stress. They lessen your burdens and help you keep things in perspective. Laughter brings your nervous system into balance, reducing stress, calming you down, sharpening your mind and making you more empathic.

Learn to see conflict as an opportunity to grow closer to others. Conflict and disagreements are inevitable in human relationships. Two people can't possibly have the same needs, opinions, and expectations at all times. However, that needn't be a bad thing. Resolving conflict in healthy, constructive ways can strengthen trust between people. When conflict isn't perceived as threatening or punishing, it fosters freedom, creativity, and safety in relationships.

www.ingramcontent.com/pod-product-compliance
Lightning Source LLC
LaVergne TN
LVHW020534160826
845677LV00015B/4052
9798846440968